Parting From The Four Attachments

Series of teachings 128 E

HIS HOLINESS SAKYA TRIZIN

Parting From The Four Attachments

Teachings given in Merigar (Italy)
25-28 June 1998

Edited by ELISA COPELLO

with the collaboration of ANDY LUKIANOWICZ

Shang Shung Publications

*Any errors are due to the transcription and translation
and do not reflect the original teachings.*

© 1999 Shang Shung Edizioni
Località Merigar
58031 Arcidosso, Italy
Tel: 0564966039
E-mail: shangshunged@tiscali.it
www.shangshungpublications.org

ISBN: 978-88-7834-120-3

Design by Kasia Skura

Contents

The Right Motivation

❖ First of all, I wish to take this opportunity to extend my very warm greetings to Chögyal Namkhai Norbu Rinpoche as well as to all the Community here and to all the people who have come to this teaching. I would also like to thank the Community very much for inviting me here and giving us such a warm reception in this beautiful place. We are very well rested and we are enjoying the weather, the scenery and everything. Today I will be giving teachings on Parting from the Four Attachments and so, before we begin the teaching, first of all, it is our tradition to recite the Lineage Gurus Prayers. We can recite it together, because I believe all of you have been distributed a copy of it.

Before we receive the teaching, the very first thing is to create the right motivation, because whenever you receive teachings or whatever practice you do, where it leads to depends on one's motivation. The motivation of course has many different levels, but if a teaching has to become a Mahayana teaching, it is very important to have or to create the higehest motivation. So the purpose of receiving teachings is not for just one's own sake but for the sake of all sentient beings as wide as space. It is in order to save them from suffering and in order to place them on the path of bliss, for the sake of all limitless sentient beings, that one must attain full enlightenment. Such enlightenment does not rise without proper cause and conditions, therefore first of all in order to attain enlightenment one must receive the holy teaching and after receiving it, whatever is mentioned in it must be diligently applied on the path. When you receive teachings, you must watch your behaviour: as far as the body is concerned you must sit in a respectful position, which means that lying down or sitting in different ways is not allowed unless you are physically handicapped. Verbally you must remain in complete silence, and mentally you must concentrate on every word of the teaching. One should listen to the teachings with great joy, free from the three faults of the container. This means that if the container is upside down, then whatever you try to pour into it, nothing goes into it. Similarly if you are sitting in this temple but your mind is distracted by other things, then you cannot hear or you cannot hold any deep meaning, so this is called the fault of the upside down container.

The second fault of the container occurs when the container is in an upright position but with a hole underneath: so whatever you pour from the top, it leaks out and nothing remains in the container. Similarly even though you hear, trying to pay attention and to remember what is being taught, you will not hold it: you hear, but you forget, that is to say that when you reach the middle of the teaching, you have forgotten the beginning and when you reach the end of the teaching, you have forgotten the middle part and by the time the teaching is over, you cannot remember anything. So this is called the second fault of the container.

Now we come to the third fault of the container: even if the container is in an upright position and there are no holes underneath, but there is dirt inside, then whatever good things you pour in it, they get spoiled by the dirt and you cannot use them. Similarly if one has faults then it is not good. Therefore not only should the container have the correct upright position with no holes, but it is also important that the container should be clean.

Which are the dirty things? There are six faults: the first one is pride about one's race, pride about one's knowledge, etc. No qualities can remain because of the fault of pride, that is why fault number one is pride.

The second fault is being disrespectful, that is to say that even though you are receiving teachings you have no faith in the teacher or in the teaching. So you are listening just to gain ordinary knowledge or out of curiosity. If you are receiving teachings in this way it is not right. The third fault is when there is no real interest in the teaching. The fourth is when your mind is distracted by outer objects or when your mind is roaming around, so that there is no real concentration on the teaching. The fifth is that, even if you are not distracted by outer objects, your mind is dull and it is inwardly sleeping, preventing you from concentrating or understanding the teaching. The sixth is being impatient, because the teaching is too long or because we have no capacity to understand it, etc. So, being free from these faults, we should receive teaching with the six intentions: we should consider the Master our spiritual teacher, like a spiritual doctor; the Dharma like medicine; ourselves like a patient; defilements (hatred, pride, attachment etc) like severe illnesses; and the practice of Dharma like a medical treatment. The sixth intention is the wish that, through the practice and because Buddha has never deceived, but, on the contrary, has always been truthful, the holy Dharma might remain in this universe forever. With these six intentions one should receive the teachings.

Thus if one is free from these faults and receives the teaching properly, then receiving the teachings itself includes all the main practices of the Bodhisattva, called the six paramitas or six perfections. The first is the perfection of generosity: in this case, from the disciple's side it implies the mandala offering and from the guru's side, giving teachings. So all this includes the perfection of generosity. The second is moral conduct, which means abstaining from negativities coming from non-virtuous deeds; so while you are receiving teachings you should refrain from negative deeds. Besides, by receiving teachings you gain knowledge about the right and wrong way, so this corresponds to moral conduct. The third is patience: while you are receiving teachings, you bear physical discomfort or whichever discomfort there might be, so in this way you practise patience. The fourth is endeavour, which is interest or enthusiasm in practising virtuous deeds, therefore listening to the teachings, or from the teacher's side explaining the teachings and from the disciple's side receiving teachings with great enthusiasm and interest. The fifth is called concentration on a single point: the mind is single-pointedly concentrated on the meaning of the teaching. So the perfection of concentration is included here. The sixth is wisdom: through words, one will be able to differentiate and understand the actual meaning and consequently gain wisdom: that is why it is called the perfection of wisdom. So, free from faults and in the right way, one should receive the teachings.

The Origin Of This Teaching

❖ This teaching, the path of all Buddhas of the past and of the future that contains all the deep meanings of all the Sutras combined in a practical way, is known as the Mind Training or Pith Instructions, presented by the great masters in the most practical way through their own experience. The history of this teaching is this. When the great Lama Sakyapa was twelve years old, his spiritual master suggested that, since he was the son of a great spiritual master he should study the teaching; however in order to study the teaching he needed first to acquire wisdom. In order to acquire wisdom, he had to practise Manjushri, the manifestation of all the Buddhas' wisdom. Sakyapa's spiritual master, Pari Lotsawa, one of the greatest translators, gave him the initiation of Manjushri and all the teachings related to Manjushri and then asked his disciple to do a meditation retreat. Actually the great Lama Sakyapa Kunga Nyingpo was fully enlightened and an emanation of both Manjushri and Avalokiteshvara combined together, but since he had taken human rebirth and had a human body, in the eyes of common people he had to follow the human way of life. So he was born as a child and then he proceeded step by step, studying, acquiring wisdom and so forth. With the help of his spiritual master he practised the Manjushri meditation for six months. In the beginning there were some signs of obstacles, which vanished through his practice of the wrathful deity known as Blue Achala*.

After completing the six months meditation, one day in his pure vision he saw Manjushri in person sitting on a jewel throne doing the teaching mudra, with two Bodhisattva attendants, one on each side. Then the main deity Manjushri gave this teaching, which is made up of four lines:

If you have attachment to this life,
   you are not a religiousperson.
If you have attachment to the world of existence,
   you do not have renunciation.
If you have attachment to your own purpose,
   you have no Enlightenment Thought (Bodhicitta).
If grasping arises, you do not have the view.

All the paths of the Sutrayana are included in these four lines. Through this practice, Lama Sakyapa gained great insight wisdom and then he gave this teaching to his sons, and since then it has been passed down from one master to the next one until now. I received it myself from a number of teachers, from my main guru as well as

---

* Wrathful form of Mahavairochana [Note by A. Lukianowicz]

from other gurus. My guru is the great Abbot No Lodro Shenpen Nyingpo. This is the history of this teaching.

The Pith Instructions

❖ Now we come to the pith instructions them-selves, which include three parts: the preliminary part, the main part and the concluding part.

I. THE PRELIMINARY PART

I.I. REFUGE

The preliminary part is subdivided into two parts. First, in order to switch from the wrong path to the right path, we take Refuge in the Buddha, Dharma and Sangha. Although taking Refuge is common to all schools of Buddhism, in Mahayana we have a special Refuge hav-ing four special characteristics. First, the way we take Refuge: we take Refuge in the Buddha who, according to Mahayana, is endowed with unimaginable qualities, is completely free from all kinds of faults and obscurations and endowed with the three Kayas (Dharmakaya, Samb-hogakaya and Nirmanakaya). Then we take Refuge in the Dharma, which has two parts: the realization and the teachings. The realization refers to the great qualities of Buddhas and Bodhisattvas who have already reached the irreversible state. Such realization and the teachings are the Dharma. Then there is Refuge in the Sangha, which in general means the community, but here it refers to the Bodhisattvas who, having already reached the irreversible state, represent the true Sangha. So the object of Mahayana teaching, of Mahayana Refuge is represented by the Buddha with the three Kayas; by the Dharma in the two aspects of realization and teachings that Buddha and the Bodhisattvas possess; and by the Sangha, that is, the Bodhisattvas who have already reached the irreversible state. This is the special object of Mahayana Refuge.

The second characteristic is the cause for taking Refuge, which includes three aspects: the fear of suffering, faith in the Triple Gem and compassion, which in Mahayana Refuge represents the main point: compassion for all sentient beings who are suffering.

The third speciality or characteristic is that we take Refuge not for a limited time, such as our life span or till we reach liberation, but until enlightenment is reached and we ourselves become Buddha. So we take Refuge in Buddha, Dharma and Sangha till we reach full enlightenment.

The fourth characteristic is that when taking Refuge, one does not take it just for oneself or one's own purpose but for the purpose of all other sentient beings without any discrimination or exception. So with these special characteristics we take Refuge, from now until enlightenment is reached, in Buddha as our guide, in Dharma as our actual path and in Sangha representing all our companions.

In this way we recite the Refuge verses many times and at the end we pray to the Triple Gem to bestow the blessings so that our mind may not be distracted by worldly activities but, on the contrary, be deeply engaged in Dharma practice. The second request we make to the Three Jewels is not only that our mind might be engaged in Dharma practice, but also that we might be successful in turning whichever practice we do into real Dharma. Then we also ask the Three Jewels to bestow their blessings so that all confusion and illusions on the path might be cleared away. Again we ask to receive their blessings so that all the illusory visions in which we are living now might turn into primordial wisdom. We make the request to receive their blessings so that no non-religious or non-dharmic thought might arise even for a single moment. Again we ask their blessings in order to attain enlightenment very quickly. All these requests have a direct connection with the main teachings, because when your mind goes deeply into Dharma you give up attachment to this life, which corresponds to the first line of the teaching. When we ask to be successful on the Dharma path, it means we give up attachment to this world, not only to this life, but to all worldly existence. The third request, directed to clear away any kind of confusion and illusion, means giving up attachment to one's own purposes. The fourth request, directed to turn illusory vision into primordial wisdom, refers to the fourth line: „If grasping arises, then you do not possess the view".

1.2. ENLIGHTENMENT THOUGHT (BODHICITTA)

The second preliminary practice consists in creating the Enlightenment Thought in order to switch from the lower path to the higher path. One should think that samsara is full of suffer-ing and that nobody wishes to have suffering, but although we have to think about other beings we have the tendency to consider ourselves as number one. So before doing anything one might think that the right way should be to attain liberation for one-self and be free from the suffering of samsara. But it is not like this, because if you attain nirvana for your own purposes, then you do not fully develop the qualities and therefore you cannot help other beings; in this way you do not fulfil either your own purposes or the purpose of others. Besides it is much harder to do all over again something you did in a wrong way than to start some-thing new from the very beginning

As far as all sentient beings are concerned, since according to the teaching our consciousness has been roaming in samsara from beginningless time, each sen-tient being has been in one life or another very close to us as a friend or a parent or a relative and so forth. Because we continuously change lives, we are no longer able to recognize each other. We see someone as a friend and we have attachment, or we consider someone as an en-emy and we develop hatred, or we are indifferent towards people we do not know, the attitude which corresponds to ignorance. Through these defilements, we are caught up in the circle of existence.

Therefore we must have feelings: for example even in a worldly way, if one is a good person and finds himself in a safe place, but his family members are suffering somewhere else, he will not feel happy about it. If you are a kind-hearted person you would rather suffer together with your own family than stay alone in a safe and happy place knowing that all the other members of your family are suffering. Therefore we must have feelings for other sentient beings: one should not just think about one's own wellbeing but should also care for the wellbeing of other sentient beings. So we must develop our compassion for other sentient beings, even if mere compassion will not help: we actually need to rescue sentient beings from suffering and lead them towards the path of happiness. At the moment we do not possess full knowledge, compassion and the power to rescue other sentient beings: we ourselves are helpless, completely conditioned by karma and defilements, and wherever the wind of karma blows we are forcedly driven there. We have no choice, so how can we help other sentient beings who are suffering? Normally even the most powerful worldly deities have not got such skill and power to rescue all sentient beings. Besides, even those who have already reached nirvana, like the Shravakas and Pratyekabuddhas, have not got the full power to rescue sentient beings. In fact the only ones who possess the full qualities, full knowledge, full compassion and full power are the Buddhas. All the Buddhas have full skills and powers enabling them to rescue sentient beings. Therefore it is for the sake of all sentient beings that one must attain full enlightenment.

We all possess Buddha nature: in all sentient beings the true nature of mind has never been stained by obscurations. Temporary obscurations blocking beings and preventing them from seeing the true nature of mind can be eliminated by the effective methods that we have. That is why it is most meaningful and beneficial to attain full enlightenment for the sake of all sentient beings. Such enlightenment does not arise without cause and condition or from the wrong cause and condition. So in order to attain enlightenment you diligently practise following this profound path, the path of all past, present and future Buddhas. In this way you create the enlightenment-thought, switching from the lower path to the higher path. Through the recitation of some verses belonging to a famous four-line prayer composed by Atisha, we take Refuge and creates the Enlightenment Thought at the same time. This is the meaning of the four lines:

I take Refuge in Buddha, Dharma and Sangha,
 the most excellent community,
Until enlightenment is reached.

This is the Refuge part. The following two lines represent the creation of the Enlightenment Thought:

By the merit of generosity and other good deeds,
May all sentient beings attain enlightenment.

So in this way you create the Enlightenment Thought through the dedication of merits. By good deeds we mean practising generosity, good moral conduct and so forth; you then dedicate the merits you have accumulated through these good deeds to the full enlightenment of all sentient beings.

These two preliminary practice verses are not directly mentioned in the main teaching, but it is obvious that in every Buddhist practice we do there is Refuge. This is because Refuge is the root of all Dharma, the preliminary practice of all paths, the foundation of all vows and what differentiates Buddhism from other teachings. That is why it is absolutely essential and obvi-ous to take Refuge, that is considered the first preliminary practice. The second preliminary practice is the creation of the Enlightenment Thought, that is the foundation of the Mahayana path and the essential base for Mahayana practitioners.

2. THE MAIN PART

The main practice includes four parts.

2.1. THE FIRST LINE

First of all you should sit in the lotus position or which-ever position may be comfortable, then you take Ref-uge and create the Enlightenment Thought. Alter that, you start the main practice. As you may remember, the first line says: „If you have attachment to this life, you are not a religious person". In fact to become a Dharma practitioner, to be in real Dharma, you must give up attachment to this life, because clinging to this life or having attachment to it is like clinging to a water mirage which will never be able to quench your thirst. Similarly, if we have attachment to this life, then whatever spiritual practice we do - such as keeping good moral conduct, studying, receiving teachings, contemplating or meditating, will just be a method used to enhance the prosperity of this life, without ever becoming real Dharma, real teaching.

How to practise Dharma? The great master Vasubandhu said that on the basis of good moral conduct one must then listen (that means study), contemplate and meditate, and this is the general structure common to all the schools: Hinayana, Mahayana, Vajrayana and so forth. In order to do this, you have to give up attachment to this life. As explained before, moral con-duct is very important if one wishes to be reborn as a human being or in the Deva realm, because it is the root of the higher realms. It is the ladder to attain liberation: in order to attain liberation it is important to have rebirth in the higher realms, so the basis for spiritual practice is moral conduct. It is the antidote in order to abandon suffering; in fact the most effective way to abandon suffering is by keeping a good moral conduct.

Although oral conduct is very important, if you keep it just for the sake of this life then instead of becoming the root of higher realms it turns into the root of the eight worldly dharmas. These are: gain and loss (gain-

ing or losing position and wealth), happiness and un-
happiness, fame and obscurity, praise and blame. Ordinary people are involved in these eight worldly dharmas:
when you gain or are happy or hear pleasant speech or are
praised you have good feelings, but when you lose or are
unhappy or hear unpleasant speech or are blamed then
you feel very bad about it. The main things the ordinary
person aims for or tries to avoid are the eight worldly
dharmas. Keeping moral conduct with attachment to this
life implies criticising those who do not keep good moral
conduct and being jealous of people who really have
good moral conduct. In that case one's own moral conduct is merely hypocrisy, appearance: such moral conduct
is not the right one and becomes the seed for a rebirth in
the lower realms. Therefore one must avoid having such
moral conduct.

Then, when we speak of listening or studying, we
refer to receiving teachings, studying and contemplating. They are very essential, because through hearing,
studying and contemplating we obtain the wealth of all
knowledge. They are the lamp that dispels the darkness
of ignorance, the knowledge of the path that leads living
beings to the right path and the seed of Dharmakaya,
because through gaining knowledge, studying and contemplating, we do meditation, we improve it and eventually we attain Dharmakaya. So study and contemplation,
or hearing and contemplating, are absolutely essential in
Dharma practice. But the person who does contemplation or studies with attachment to this life will obtain
the opposite result: he will attain worldly pride, because

when you get knowledge, you feel very proud of it. This person will look down on other people who are not so good at studying and contemplating and on the other hand he will be jealous of those who possess the capacity of hearing and contemplating. Then one starts seeking followers and wealth and so in this way hearing and contemplating become the root for rebirth in the lower realms. Hearing and contemplating completely involved with the eight worldly dharmas are not right and consequently you have to put aside this way of hearing and contemplating.

Then we have meditation, which is very important because it is the direct antidote, the most effective way to eliminate defilements. It is the root for reaching the path of liberation and is the seed for attaining Buddhahood. Meditation is the essence of the path of spiritual practice, but again the person who meditates with attachment to this life will attain the opposite effect, and even if he remains in a secluded place he is still busy and involved in worldly activities. In this way reciting and chanting prayers results in blind chanting of words, and such a person criticises those who are involved in studying and contemplating because he considers that only meditation is important, and at the same time he is jealous of people who do meditation. One's own meditation is full of distraction, and such meditation linked to the eight worldly dharmas is not right, so we have to put it aside.

So this first line, saying that if you have attachment to this life you are not a religious person, directly differentiates the right way of practising Dharma from the wrong way, and by avoiding the wrong way one must try to practise Dharma in a right way.

Indirectly this line tells you that in order to realize the need and the importance of practising Dharma in your life you must meditate on how difficult it is to obtain the precious human life. Besides, it is important not only to practise Dharma in our life but also to speed up practice without any delay, meditating on impermanence and death. First of all, one must reflect on the difficulty of obtaining precious human life, because in order to practise Dharma you need a base. Although all sentient beings possess Buddha nature and every sentient being has the potential to become a Buddha, human beings really have this possibility and the best chance. In order to have the base for Dharma practice it is very important to obtain human life in general and in particular human life endowed with eighteen prerequisites. Why is it difficult to obtain human life? It can be explained from many points of view: first of all from the cause point of view: because to obtain ordinary human life in general you must have done virtuous deeds and in particular you must have kept good moral conduct. Special human life endowed with the eighteen prerequisites is the result of very many virtuous deeds, correct moral conduct and very strong prayers, without which this special human life would be impossible to obtain. When we examine ourselves and the whole universe surrounding us, we notice that in general there are very few people who practise virtuous deeds, and even those who are sup-posed to practise them do it at a very superficial level. In fact those who practise virtuous deeds and keep good moral conduct are very rare, therefore since the cause concerns very few people, the result will be that human life is difficult to obtain.

From the number point of view, it is said in the Sutra teachings that the sentient beings falling down from higher to lower realms are as many as the atoms of this universe, while sentient beings going up from lower to higher realms are as few as dust specks on one's own thumb nail. Even if there are many human beings and we talk about the population explosion, if we compare them to other living beings human beings are much fewer in number: in fact you can easily count how many human beings live in a country, but it is very hard to count how many insects live in a small house! From the example point of view, there is a famous example which can be found in the Sutras as well as in some main commentaries. Suppose that the whole universe is like a big ocean where there is a golden yoke with only one hole floating on the surface, and there a blind turtle residing on the bottom of the ocean which comes to the surface once every a hundred years. Since the golden yoke floats on the vast surface of the ocean pushed here and there by winds and the turtle is blind and comes up only every a hundred years, it is extremely difficult for the turtle to slip its neck into the yoke hole. This example bears a great similarity to our own situation: the ocean is wide and big, similarly the possibilities of being reborn as other (not human) living beings are vast. The small hole in the golden yoke symbolises the very few chances we have to be reborn as human beings. The turtle coming to the surface of the ocean once every a hundred years symbolises the people who are practising and creating the cause for a human rebirth, which is very rare. The blindness of the turtle symbolises that also the creation of the cause for a human rebirth is not strong but very weak. The golden yoke floating on the surface everywhere according to the direction of winds blowing eastwards or westwards means that even those creating the cause for a human rebirth have many obstacles which can block this possibility.

From the nature point of view, human life endowed with all the eighteen prerequisites is very difficult to obtain, which means that one is free from the eight unfavourable places and has the ten favourable conditions. Among the eight unfavourable places, four are represented by the non-human states and four are within the human state.

The first non-human state is hell: if one is born in the hell realm, not only is there a lot of suffering, there is also no way to receive the teaching, so there is no chance to practise Dharma. The second is the hungry ghost realm: here again there is so much hunger and thirst that there is no way to practise Dharma. The third is the animal realm: by animals we intend all other living beings apart from human beings, like mammals, birds and so forth we see around us. All animals have great ignorance: it is as if they all had a huge rock placed on top of their heads and that is why it is impossible for them to understand the difference between right and wrong. Besides, they do not feel any shame and consequently they cannot practise Dharma. The fourth is the realm of long-living gods: some commentaries say that in general for all the ordinary gods living in the heavenly realm, indulging in luxury and engaged in entertainment, there is no way to practise. They say that in one particular part of the heavenly realm within the realm of form, there is a section where the long-living gods reside. From birth until death all their mental activities cease and they remain in a kind of complete inactive state, so in such a place there is no chance to practise Dharma.

Among the four places within the human realm, the first one is the place of barbarians who have no way to receive instructions on what should be done and what one should abstain from: there is no way to meet a spiritual guide who can give these instructions. In the second, even if they have the chance of receiving instructions, people have wrong views: they do not believe that liberation arises from virtuous deeds and suffering arises from non-virtuous deeds, they do not believe in the law of karma or in the Triple Gem and so forth. The third is to be born in a time when Buddha has not manifested in this universe: if he has not come, there is no Dharma to practise. The fourth one is represented by people who have defects in their organs, like dumb or mentally handicapped people: for mentally handicapped people there is no way to receive instructions and consequently to practise Dharma.

So these are the eight unfavourable places or conditions. We are fortunate not to have been born in such unfavourable places, because when we consider other living beings the majority of them are in one of these unfavourable places.

Besides being free from these eight unfavourable places we are endowed with ten favourable conditions, of which five come from our own side and five from outside. The five to obtain from our own side are the following:

To be born as a human being.

To be born in a centrally located place, which has two meanings: centrally located geographically and in terms of Dharma. Geographically centrally located refers to a place like Bodhgaya in India, where all past, present and future Buddhas obtain enlightenment. Dharmically centrally located refers to a place where there are the four types of Buddha's followers: monks and nuns and male and female lay followers.

To be endowed with sound organs, enabling us easily to receive instructions and understand the meaning of Dharma.

To have unshakeable faith in Buddha's teaching in general and in particular in the Vinaya, the root of Dharma.

To have never committed extreme actions: the five heavy crimes (killing one's father or mother, killing an Arhat, spilling the blood of a Buddha, creating disharmony inside the Sangha). If one has commit one or more of these heavy crimes oneself or has asked other people to commit them or has supported them in some way there is generally no chance for this person to practise

Dharma, although in the higher path it is possible. So these are the five favourable conditions which you need to obtain from your own side.

Then we have the other five conditions which arise from outside:

To be born at a time when Buddha has come. It is very rare for a Buddha to come to this universe. When he comes we have a light aeon and when he does not come, we have a dark aeon. Fortunately in this aeon thousands of Buddhas have come, so we are in a fortunate aeon, but generally we have many more dark aeons than light aeons. After many dark aeons, there are one or two light aeons, therefore most of the time we are in a dark aeon. Even during a light aeon, when people's life length is increasing, a Buddha may not come, therefore most of the time Buddha does not come.

The second condition is that not only has Buddha come but he also turns the wheel of Dharma: Buddha does not turn the wheel of Dharma when there are no followers worthy to receive teachings. Historically, when Buddha Shakyarmuni attained enlightenment under the bodhi tree at Bodhgaya he said that he had found the nectar but he did not want to bestow it, because there was no one who could understand it, so he would remain there without turning the wheel of Dharma. Then Lord Brahma offered him a golden wheel with a thousand spokes, making him the request to turn the wheel of Dharma, and only then did Buddha accept and turn the wheel of Dharma.

The third condition is that the teaching is still a living tradition: many Buddhas come but there may be long gaps between one Buddha and the next, during which the teachings might get lost. That is why it is important that one should be born in a time when the teaching is still alive.

The fourth condition is that even if the teaching is still a living tradition, there are very few people following it. As you can see, there are many other beings who do not practise Dharma or follow the teaching, and even among those who do follow the teachings, instead of practising true Dharma many are merely following it in appearance. Therefore very few people enter the Dharma path, so not only it is important to be born when the teaching is still alive but also to enter the right Dharma path.

The fifth condition is that it should be easy for Dharma practitioners to find proper livelihood. For superficial practitioners it is easy to find the right livelihood, while for serious Dharma practitioners residing in a very secluded place like on a high mountain or in the jungle, it is difficult to obtain proper livelihood. In fact when the great Milarepa was in meditation he had difficulties in finding food, so to have the opportunity for serious practitioners to find the right livelihood is the fifth condition.

Therefore human life endowed with all the eighteen prerequisites is extremely rare from many points of view, and is more precious than the wish-fulfilling jewel. In fact if you address a prayer to the wish-fulfilling jewel it can provide you with material things like food, clothes, shelter, medicines and so forth but it cannot bestow higher rebirth, personal liberation or en-lightenment. Through having this human life it is possible to attain higher re-birth, personal liberation and ultimately full enlighten-ment, using this life as a vehicle. That is why this life is not only rare but is also very precious indeed. So when we have such a precious and rare opportunity, if we lose this chance there is no greater loss than missing this op-portunity. When you realize how rare and precious it is, you should not remain idle, you should think about how to utilize it, realizing that the best way is the practice of Dharma. By reflecting on the preciousness of human life and the difficulty of obtaining it, the need to prac-tise Dharma arises together with the awareness of how important it is to devote oneself to practice in this very lifetime. Then one should reflect on impermanence and death and be aware of how important it is to practise Dharma without any delay.

Generally speaking, all Buddhist teachings say that all compounded things are impermanent, all things aris-ing from causes and conditions are impermanent. As for our life, what is one hundred per cent sure is that anyone who is born to this life in this world is bound to die: everyone who is born to this life in this world will meet death. Wherever you search, there is no place in samsara that death cannot reach. There is not even any slightest doubt about the fact that everyone who is born must die: anyone who is born meets death at the end. In the eyes of common people even fully enlightened Buddhas who are totally free from death and birth apparently enter into mahaparanirvana, but for we ordinary people, one thing which is absolutely certain in our life is that one day we have to face death. There are many causes and conditions that can cut our life, while there are very few conditions which can prolong it and even conditions meant to prolong our life like medicine and food, can sometimes cause death if we take the wrong medicine or food.

Meditating on impermanence implies first of all reflecting on the certainty of death and then on the uncertainty about when death will strike. Some people die even before being born, some soon after birth, some during childhood and some others during adolescence and so forth: since there is no definite life span, death can strike at any time and anywhere. The third thing is that at the time of death, nothing can help us, no matter how rich, powerful and learned we are or how many religious friends we have: nothing can help and we have to face death by ourselves. The only thing we can hold on to, the only thing that can save and help us is the holy Dharma: so while we are still living, young and healthy, without wasting time, we must practise Dharma. Through the practice of Dharma, the best practitioners at the time of death have no fear, because it is like going to a known destination. Practitioners of medium capacity who have practised in their lifetime have no hesitation. Inferior practitioners who have practised in their lifetime at least have no regret. Through meditation on impermanence, one is aware not only of the importance of practising Dharma but also of the importance of practising it without any delay. We may say: "When we are young, we

can do other things, then when we get older we can devote ourselves to Dharma practice," or: "This year I will
do other things, next year I will practise Dharma:" but if
we postpone practice in this way we will never know if
we will have such a chance or not. Consequently without
any delay we must practise Dharma diligently. In this way
we have completed the first line of the teaching.

2.2. THE SECOND LINE

The second line says: "If you have attachment to this
worldly existence, you do not have renunciation". With
attachment to worldly existence you are not on the path
leading to enlightenment: that is why one must give up
attachment to worldly existence. The world of existence,
wherever you might be, always has the nature of suffering.
If we want proper renunciation to arise it is important
to remember the suffering of samsara or of the world
of existence. According to the teaching there are three
types of suffering in samsara: the suffering of suffering,
the suffering of change and the suffering of the conditioned nature of all things. Suffering of suffering means
the suffering we normally consider as such, like physical
pain, mental anxiety, worries and so forth: this suffering
is mainly in the lower realms. If we carefully meditate
on this, this suffering is unbearable: one's physical body
could be trembling and shaking, and if one were forced
to bear such suffering there would be no way to stand it.
For example, even now a tiny bit of fire scorching our
body or a tiny needle piercing it can cause great pain: in

the lower realms beings are burning, on fire, and there are different kinds of weapons piercing their bodies, so how can a being bear all this? The situation is such that if we do not practise virtuous deeds and instead plant the seed to fall down into the lower realms the result will be pitiful for us. Then if we reflect on the suffering of change, this refers to what I said at the beginning: there are many beings falling down from the higher realms to the lower ones. Even the king of Devas, who was born in such a high position, falls down as well taking rebirth as a very poor, ordinary person. Like the sun and moon which are very bright and give light to the whole universe because of their position, one could find oneself in this dimension of light and then subsequently be born in a totally dark place where one cannot even see one's own hands. In ancient times there were universal emperors who ruled over many continents because of their high and powerful position, but then they would take rebirth as ordinary servants. All these things are clearly mentioned in Buddha's teaching, but we are ordinary persons unable to understand them directly, because we cannot see the hell realm, the god realm, etc. Therefore the easiest way to understand the suffering of change is to examine our human situation: rich people becoming very poor, powerful persons becoming weak, a family with many members dying out, etc.

Then if you reflect on the suffering of the conditioned nature of all things, this means that whatever we do is suffering and there is no end to it, no matter how hard we work and how much effort we do, there is no end to our actions. There is suffering when there are many people and suffering when there are few people, when you are rich at the material level or when you are poor, no matter where you are, what you do, who you associate with, all is suffering. We are busy and always deceived by our activities. Then we die and even after death there is no end to actions. Again we enter into the busy life of our next life, so wherever we are as long as we are still in samsara or the world of existence there is no real peace or happiness: anyone caught up in samsara is in a pitiful situation. In this way the second line shows directly the suffering of samsara and indirectly the relationship between cause and effect or the law of karma: the reason why we are born in samsara is becouse of self-indulgence in our own karma.

Speaking about the suffering of samsara in greater detail, we have to say that sarnsara is divided in six realms: the lower realms consisting in the hell, hungry ghost and animal realms, and the higher realms, consisting in the human, demigod and god realms. All these realms have suffering and the suffering of suffering, what we normally consider as physical pain, mental torture, worries, anxiety, etc. This mainly concerns the three lower realms. The hell realms are mainly divided into three types: the cold hells, the hot hells and the neighbouring and similar hells. In the cold hells there are blizzards and ice, not even a single star is shining, all is in total darkness and there are no clothes to protect oneself from the cold. As we said, the cold hells are characterised by blizzards and snow storms: altogether there are eight different types of cold hells. Besides, one does not stay in the cold hells for a short time but for an unimaginable length of time. Then in the eight hot hells persons are on a burning iron ground, surrounded by burning fire and tortured by all kinds of weapons cutting and piercing the body for a very long period of time. The neighbouring hells are smaller, but there is much suffering in them and they surround the main hot hells. In these hells, beings and animals are cut, boiled and tortured in many ways. The similar hells are like our human realm where animals are boiled alive in hot water or burnt on fire.

Then we have the second lower realm of hungry ghosts, conditioned by stinginess and greed: one is born in such a poor place that there is not even a single grain or a drop of water but only the total suffering of hunger and thirst in a desert of dust. There are three different types: outer obscurations, inner obscurations and the obscurations of obscurations. Outer obscurations refer to places where there is no food, no drink, and the beings have an ugly appearance with a huge stomach, a tiny throat and a very tiny mouth and so forth. Inner obscurations mean that on top of this suffering, when these beings sometimes find very dirty food like mucus etc., first of all they have such a tiny mouth that food cannot get inside, and even if they succeed in putting it into their mouth, they have such a tiny throat that the food cannot get through or it becomes so rough as to make the throat sore and in the end, if by any chance it reaches the stomach, which is as huge as a mountain, it does not satisfy their hunger and instead brings more hunger and thirst. The obscurations of obscurations mean that the hungry ghosts are constantly dragging their bodies even though they are physically weak: because of the suffering of hunger, they drag them all over the place and when they find some food, other powerful beings chase them away and beat them. Even if they have found a tiny piece of bad food, they cannot take it. Sometimes they manage to save it, but they suffer while it is passing through their mouth and throat, and even if food moves down to the stomach, it becomes fire and burns inwardly. This suffering lasts for thousands and thousands of years.

The third lower realm is the animal realm. Animals are considered to be all other living beings which are not human, that is to say different types of fish, birds, mammals, insects, etc., which are included in this realm. There are two main divisions: beings living in the big ocean and those scattered around in different places. Animals dwelling in the great ocean are very many, and because of big ocean waves they are driven to different places where they always meet different companions, so that not even for a single moment can they relax, on the contrary small fish are afraid of being eaten by huge fish and big fish of being attacked by a swarm of small fish. Animals scattered around in many different places fall into two categories: animals belonging to human beings, which carry heavy loads or plough huge fields, are milked, tied up, or hit with a stick. They undergo all kinds of torture and must work all their life without any possibility of retirement such as human beings have.

At the end, instead of retiring from work they are killed for their flesh, skin and bones or sold to somebody else: they really have to bear all these kinds of tortures. Then there are wild animals living on the mountains and so forth. They do not reside in a definite permanent place but are always roaming around, they never know when and if they are going to meet enemies or be attacked by human beings or other animals. Hunters might hit them to eat them, or such animals might only be injured and forced to run away to a safe place. They have to bear so much suffering. In general animals have great ignorance as if they had a huge stone placed on top of their head: there is no way for them to understand what is right or wrong. When we think about the suffering of all the three lower realms, if we had to bear such suffering, there would be no way to bear it, but there is no guarantee that we will not be born in such a place. The cause for rebirth in these three lower realms is indulging in the mental defilements of hatred, greed and ignorance even for a single day. That is why it is very likely for all of us to fall down into the lower realms. Therefore, by understanding that, we must have the strong will to practise Dharma so that we will be able to divert from the road leading to the lower realms and not take rebirth in them.

As for the suffering of change, which means falling down from the higher realms, we have a feeling that we normally consider as a happy feeling if it is compared to suffering, but in reality this is not happiness but just another type of suffering. For example, if a person who is in a very poor condition, in a house that is cold in winter, hot in summer and wet in the rainy season, smelly, filthy etc., moves to a luxurious house with all facilities, of course he feels happy because of all the comforts he then has compared to the ones available in his previous place. If these facilities are the real cause of happiness, the more you stay in such a comfortable place the happier you should be, but again if you happen to live in that place for a very long time you will feel unhappy and wish to go elsewhere: this proves that in appearance facilities seem to be the cause of happiness but in reality they are another type of suffering.

Then in our life, in the dimension of human beings, no one is free from the four types of sufferings of birth, old age, sickness and death. Then we are afraid of meeting enemies, of parting from our dear ones, of not being able to fulfil our wishes, of having to cope with a lot of undesirable events, etc.: everything turns into so much suffering! Very powerful people with a position of prestige have a big fall and become very weak, and rich people become very poor. In the human realm there is so much suffering that there is no need to give further explanations: everybody knows very well that in the world we live in there is no satisfaction or real happiness.

The second higher realm of the demigods or asuras is dominated by jealousy. They never feel equal to the gods and consequently they are constantly engaged in battles against them. Since they have accumulated fewer merits than the gods they are always defeated: the male demigods, husbands, fathers, etc. are killed on battlefields while the mothers and wives stay at home waiting, and they hear bad news concerning their male companions, so there is also this type of suffering.

In the third higher realm, the dimension of the gods, because of good previous karma the gods live in a beautiful place, enjoy a good food and have all the luxuries and pleasures one could think of. Life for them is full of pleasure, which however is not permanent so, when their time is due, then physical and mental signs of death occur and they know they are going to die. Because their whole life has been wasted in pleasure and enjoyment of different kinds, they are aware they will fall down into the lower realms and consequently they experience mental agony and suffering greater than the physical pains a being has to bear in the hell realms.

Then there are the dimensions of much higher gods residing in the world of form and in the world without form. They have not got any kind of visible suffering and they reach a very high state. But just like a bird which, no matter how high it might fly in the sky, eventually has to touch ground, similarly no matter how high they might be, when their worldly meditation state eventually is exhausted they fall down into the lower realms. Therefore in the whole of samsara, no matter where one is born, there is not even a single tiny place worthy of attachment. Even if one is born in a very high state of samsara one is not free from suffering. Just like poison put into food makes it harmful no matter how good or bad that food might be, similarly no matter where one is born, either in the lower or higher realms, the dimension of one's birth is worthless. So in this time during this life one should develop the strong will to totally abandon attachment to the world of existence in order to take at least some steps towards enlightenment.

Meditation on the conditioned nature of all things concerns neutral feelings of indifference presenting neither happiness nor suffering, which in reality are suffering as well. Actually our very existence itself is suffering: no matter where you are, whom you associate with, if you are in a rich or in a poor country, if you are with relatives, friends or enemies, there are no satisfaction and real peace, so wherever you are, there is always suffering. To reflect on cause and effect or the law of karma we have to ask ourselves why we have to face all the sufferings of samsara I have just described. The cause of all our sufferings is self-indulgence in non-virtuous deeds. If one wishes to be free from such suffering it is important to avoid the cause of suffering. Generally speaking there are three types of actions: virtuous, non-virtuous and indifferent or neutral deeds. For example, to understand what we mean by non-virtuous deeds, if there is poison in the root of a tree then whatever grows on it - leaves, fruit, etc. - is poisonous. Similarly, actions arising from defilements like attachment to people who are on our own side and hatred towards others, and ignorance are generally known as non-virtuous deeds.

If we want to examine negative actions more in detail, there are ten non-virtuous deeds. The first three ones are committed with the body. The first non-virtuous deed is killing other be-ings, from tiny insects to human beings, through hatred, desire or ignorance, taking their life either directly or indirectly. The second non-virtuous deed is stealing, from tiny bits to precious things, either forcefully, quietly, or through cheating or using various methods to take away other people's belongings. The third is sexual misconduct which means to indulge in sexual activities with people who are not our life partners; even engaging in sexual activities with one's own partner in the wrong place or at a wrong time are considered to be sexual misconduct.

Then there are four non-virtuous deeds committed through speech, out of desire, hatred, etc. The first is telling lies and not telling the truth in order to cheat others. The second is saying words meant to create disharmony among individuals or groups in order to separate people who are on good terms. The third is saying very harsh, rude words out of anger, etc. so that just on hearing these words others suffer and are in pain. The fourth is what is called idle talk, that is to say words which do not bring any benefits and on the contrary create more hatred, desire, etc. Then there are three non-virtuous deeds committed with the mind. The first, that comes from desire, is that when you see other people having prosperity, a good position and very nice things you wish you could have the same for yourself. The second, that comes from anger, is wishing for somebody to suffer, die or be involved in a disaster. The last is called wrong view of ignorance you do not believe in cause and the law of karma, in the Triple Gem, in the Dharma or in the fact that happiness arises from virtuous deeds and suffering arise from non-virtuous deeds. If you do not believe in this then you have a wrong view.

By indulging in such non-virtuous deeds one has to bear the fruit and the results of these actions. There are three different types of result. The first is the result of ripening, which means that the consequence of indulging in non-virtuous deeds brings about falling into one of the three lower realms, according to the amount of non-virtuous deeds one has accumulated. If the amount is very large one will fall into the hell realm, if it is medium the fall is into the hungry ghost realm, if small, into the animals realm. Also, it all depends on one's intention: for example if you kill your enemy out of anger the result is very severe and you fall down into the hell realm; if you kill animals out of desire of their flesh, bones, skin, horns, etc., because you want all this for yourself then you will fall into the hungry ghost realm. Killing any beings out of ignorance, like children killing insects just for playing, will cause one to fall into the animal realm.

The second result includes the result similar to the cause and the result which is like a habit. The result similar to the cause means, for example, that one who has engaged in killing, even if he does not fall into the three lower realms will have a very short or unhealthy life. A person engaging in stealing will have problems with his properties, and a person engaging in sexual misconduct will have a very unhappy marriage, etc. The result which is like a habit means that by indulging in negative deeds, like killing, people will have a natural tendency to kill, to enjoy fishing, hunting etc., developing a natural liking for these things and consequently continuously creating negative karma and more causes for suffering.

The third result is called the result of ownership, which is in relation to the place where one is born. People who have indulged in negative deeds will be born in poor places where lots of natural calamities occur, like earthquakes, floods and droughts, and different types of suffering depending on non-virtuous deeds that one has committed. In short, negative, non-virtuous deeds associated with the three defilements are the cause of all suffering. Nobody wants to suffer, so if you want to avoid suffering you should have the strong will not to indulge in non-virtuous deeds. So, mentally you should have strong will and come to the strong resolution to abstain both physically and verbally from negative deeds.

As for virtuous deeds, if the root of a tree is medicine, then anything growing on that tree is medicine as well. Similarly, actions performed without hatred, desire and ignorance are called virtuous deeds, which can be divided into ten different ones. The ten virtuous deeds are the opposite of the non-virtuous ones, such as abstaining from killing, stealing etc. Here again there are three different types of result: the result of ripening implies that one is reborn in the higher realms, the second result includes the result similar to the cause and the habit-forming result. The result similar to the cause means that, by refraining from killing, one will have a long healthy life, by refraining from stealing one will have prosperity, by abstaining from sexual misconduct one will have a happy marriage etc. The habit-forming result implies that, by abstaining from killing in this life, in the next life one will have the natural tendency not to kill etc. The ownership result means that ,because of the virtuous deeds performed in the past life, one will be born in a place free from natural calamities, a rich prosperous place with abundance of fruit trees, crops etc. Since virtuous deeds are the source of all happiness and good things, one should try to make a habit of performing good deeds.

As far as neutral or indifferent actions are concerned, these actions, such as eating, walking, sitting etc., do not fall intoeither of the two categories of virtuous or non-virtuous deeds.

Since they do not produce any negative results they are far better than non-virtuous deeds, but since they do not create any positive result, performing them is like wasting time. However, by changing intention or motivation, through skilful means you can transform indifferent actions into virtuous deeds. For example, when you are eating you should think that through food you keep alive and prolong your life in order to devote your lime and energy to practising virtuous deeds. When you are walking, you may think you are going to see your spiritual master or are going to listen to Dharma teachings or you may think that on your right side there are all the Buddhas and Bodhisattvas so that you are doing a circumambulation, etc. By changing motivation through such skilful means you will transform these indifferent neutral actions into virtuous deeds. In this way the suffering of samsara and cause and effect have been explained.

2.3. THE THIRD LINE

The third line says that if you have attachment to your own purpose, you do not have the Enlightenment Thought. When one is free from attachment one can attain nirvana and experience bliss. Nevertheless liberation only of oneself is not beneficial, because all sentient beings are directly or indirectly connected with us. Even our existence in this life is due to the kindness and love bestowed on us by other people. For example if our parents and friends did not look after us as soon as we were born we would not be able to do anything and we would he like insects; instead we are able to survive because of their love and kindness. Even now as adults we always have to depend on the help of relatives, friends and so forth. Then especially when we grow older we are more and more dependent on other people, therefore every sentient being, not only present friends and relatives, but also enemies and people creating obstacles, are to be considered as dear friends and relatives as well. Thus ignoring other beings who are very close, like parents, relatives and friends, and thinking only of our own benefit and happiness, is very pitiful. The very special activity of the Bodhisattva is to take all others' suffering and misery upon himself and totally give his own merits, benefits and happiness to other sentient beings. Therefore you dedicate all your merits and blessings to other sentient beings so that they might attain enlightenment.

This indirectly shows meditation on loving kindness and compassion and directly shows the result of meditating on loving kindness and compassion, which consists in doing this exchange meditation, that is giving happiness to others and taking their sufferings upon yourself. If one realizes that samsara is full of suffering and personally attains nirvana or liberation, like the Shravakas or Pratyekabuddhas who reach a stage where the qualities are not yet fully developed, one cannot benefit others. Looking for personal liberation is the greatest obstacle for one's own full enlightenment. In order to benefit yourself as well as others the goal you must aim at is full enlightenment, which does not arise without cause and conditions or from incomplete or wrong causes. Therefore enlightenment must have its very special cause and condition: the main cause is compassion and the root of enlightenment is Bodhicitta or Enlightenment Thought. The condition is that through skilful means one reaches one's goal.

Before starting the practice of compassion first of all we have to practise loving kindness, which is the kind of love a mother has for her children. Although all of us have a certain amount of loving kindness for our children, relatives and so forth, this loving kindness is rather limited, because it is only directed towards relatives, friends, etc. This love is based on selfish thoughts: you love a person because he or she is a relative or a friend and so forth. Here when we talk about loving kindness we are referring to universal love directed not only to friends and relatives but also to enemies and people who are total strangers and unknown to us. This means all the beings in the world, without any kind of prejudice and discrimination. This is the kind of loving kindness we should try to develop.

For us ordinary persons it is difficult to start practising this kind of loving kindness towards every sentient being straight away. According to the pith instructions we have to proceed step by step: first of all you have to practise the loving kindness which is easy for you, such as what you feel for your own mother or father, relatives, friends or whoever is close to you. You have to remember all the kinds of physical, mental, material kindness these particular persons have shown to you and all the benefits and help you have received from them. Then actual loving kindness is the wish that these persons might be happy and have the cause of happiness; then applying various methods you must generate the Enlightenment Thought, reciting prayers with the strong resolution that through these prayers you might succeed in practising loving kindness. Then once you have practised well and are sure of your loving kindness towards these persons you should expand this feeling to other friends, relatives, neighbours and so forth. At the same time you should practise loving kindness towards more difficult objects such as enemies and people who have been obstacles for you. Because we are continuously changing our lives we do not recognize one another, and by hurting each other we create more suffering on both sides: that is why this time, in our present life we must control our anger through the practice of loving kindness. Eventually we must train ourselves to practise loving kindness towards all sentient beings without any kind of discrimination.

When one is well trained in this practice, through the power of loving kindness compassion arises.

Compassion means focusing on sentient beings who are suffering, expressing the wish that these beings might be free from both suffering and the cause of suffering. Also the practice of compassion implies proceeding step by step: at first you take into consideration a person who is close to you, and realizing how he has been kind to you, you generate compassion towards him until, because of your practice, natural compassion rises. Then, as explained before, you expand your practice wider until you practise compassion towards enemies and eventually towards all sentient beings. When you have developed loving kindness and compassion properly this practice helps the arising of relative Bodhicitta or relative Enlightenment Thought, which means totally devoting time and energy to the benefit of all sentient beings. The great master Shantideva said: "All the suffering in this world, in this universe, comes from the wish to obtain happiness, and all the happiness in this universe arises from wishing other people may be happy".

The difference in the result is that Buddhas and Bodhisattvas who have totally devoted themselves to the benefit of all sentient beings have accomplished their own purpose as well as the purpose of other beings. As ordinary beings, life after life we are always caring for ourselves, always concerned about our own happiness, and the result is continuous suffering. The essence of Bodhisattva activity is to practise the exchange meditation, which means to pray to take upon yourself all the physical suffering, mental anxiety and undesirable things of all sentient beings as wide as space, in order to destroy selfish thoughts that come from clinging to oneself. All the benefits, virtuous deeds, happiness and good things you possess should be freely given to all sentient beings without any kind of attachment. By saying this verbally you practise it mentally and the result is that you crush the clinging to the self, the very source of all misery and suffering in this universe. All suffering comes from selfish thoughts, which in this way are totally destroyed. Then one should practise the six perfections to ripen one's own mind and other people's mind, as well as the four collecting actions, that is to say all the general Bodhisattva activities described in the Bodhisattvacharyavatara, which should be studied and applied.

2.4. The Fourth Line

The fourth line says that if grasping arises, you do not possess the view, because the true view is away from all kinds of grasping. As long as there is grasping there is no liberation: if you grasp the concept that all phenomena are self-existing there is no liberation and not even the possibility of being reborn in higher realms. So the true view is away from any kind of grasp-ing, it is away from the concepts of the existence and non-existence of phenomena, which are considered to be extreme views. If you grasp the concept that all things exist in themselves there is no liberation and you fall into eternalism: on the other hand, if you grasp the concept that everything is nonexistent you fall into nihilism. The extremes we grasp are not the right view. Since grasping the extremes is not the right view and is, in itself, another extreme, you should joyfully remain in non-duality. This is the explanation of how to avoid the extreme views of eternalism and nihilism and how to remain in non-duality. It says here that all phenomena are a projection of one's own mind and that one should not seek a creator outside: there is no outer force or creator of all phenomena. One should remain joyfully in the natural state of mind. This explains the common view of the two Mahayana Schools: the Mind Only School and the Madhyamika School. What has been explained up to here belongs to the Mind Only School.

Then according to the special view of Madhyamika or The Middle Way School, all the visions we have are illusions or a magical show rising from interdependent origination. Things do not exist independently, they all rise from cause and effect, and when cause and effect get together, things appear; conversely, when there is no meeting point between cause and effect, things do not appear. Consequently all the things we see have an interdependent origination. When we use our sharp mind to examine how it is, we cannot draw any conclusion and we cannot describe it in one way or another because it is inexpressible. There is no discrepancy between vision arising from interdependent origination and emptiness: they are inseparable and so one should remain in this inexpressible state of non-duality.

This way directly shows how to meditate on insight wisdom, through which one recognises outer visions as mind, all mental visions as magical illusions and all phenomena as devoid of self-existing nature: in fact everything arises from interdependent origination and at the same time is inexpressible. Indirectly it explains that the base of insight wisdom is concentration. If relative Bodhicitta arises in a person, as long as there is still grasping he falls into these two extreme views. As an antidote against clinging to things by considering them real and self-existing you have to meditate on two things: concentration and insight wisdom.

Because our mind is deceived by so many thoughts, extreme thoughts, absolute Bodhicitta cannot arise in our busy mind so the first step is to bring this busy mind to single-pointed concentration. In a very secluded place, free from all kinds of disturbances, you take Refuge and create the Enlightenment Thought. Then sit in the meditation posture: for beginners it is easier to do concentration on a specific object like an image of Buddha, placing it in front of you. The image of Buddha placed in front of you reminds you of Buddha, which is a great merit as well. By doing this your mind, your eyes, your breath are all brought together on this object, and whatever distraction or thought arises, try to bring your mind back to your concentration object. By doing this practice continuously for a very long period of time you can remain single-pointedly on the concentration object, reaching a complete calm-abiding state. This alone is not enough, but it is the base: to eradicate the root of all de-filements, we need wisdom or, in other words, we need to realize the true nature of mind, which is away from the extremes of existence and non-existence, of both or nei-ther etc. Concentration is actually a method that enables you to remain stable on one single point. Through such a method, that is to say by remaining in single-pointed concentration, later on you can realize meditation on in-sight wisdom.

In order to be able to meditate on insight wisdom you need to go step by step. The first step is to under-stand that outer objects, outer visions, are mental visions. All the phenomena we see, the life we go through, all things, do not appear without a cause. All phenomena are not the creation of a force coming from outside, they arise from our own mind and propensities. When a seed planted in our mind ripens, we move from life to life, so there is no outer creator, no outer projector other than our own mind. The second step is to recognize that all mental visions are magical illusions: all things we see now or the life we go through are like a magical show or like a dream. For example, in our dreams we can visit many different countries, we can meet many different beings, we may have very sad or happy dreams, nightmares and all kind of experiences. When you wake up, not even one tiny trace remains of all of the things you saw in your dreams. Similarly our life itself is like a dream or like a reflection in a mirror: nothing is real, all is a magical illu-sion. The third step is to realize that all magical illusions are devoid of self-nature. From the relative point of view, in the various lives we go through, visions never cease, and even though they are the result of cause and effect we never perceive the interdependent origination of visions. However, by means of very careful investigation one cannot find anything real, not even one tiny bit. All is emptiness, and although vision and emptiness seem to be in contradiction, there is no discrepancy between the two because emptiness and the interdependent origination of all visions are inseparable.

To practise concentration and insight wisdom combined together you remain in single-pointed concentration and you realize together wisdom and the true nature of all phenomena. If you meditate for a very long period of time you get used to it, and then through this view natural compassion for all sentient beings who do not realize this view arises spontaneously. In this way you give up clinging to illusions and all illusory visions turn into primordial wisdom. One will be able to attain Buddhahood endowed with the three kayas.

3. THE CONCLUDING PART

Now we have the conclusion that is found in every session of practice as well as at the end every teaching. We dedicate whatever virtuous deeds we may have accumulated through listening, reflecting and meditating so that all sentient beings may attain enlightenment. I have given you this teaching that comes directly from Manjushri, the essence of all the Sutras, the complete path of the l Paramitayana, that I myself received from various teachers. These practices are very important, and until you have actually had the experience you must contemplate and meditate on each different subject. Basic teachings, such as loving kindness and the things I have described, are important foundations in order to practise very high teachings. Without them one cannot receive high teachings. Similarly in order to build skyscrapers, you must have a stable foundation. Therefore to end this teaching we will recite the mandala offering verses and the dedication prayer.ing to pay attention and to remember what is being taught, you will not hold it: you hear, but you forget, that is to say that when you reach the middle of the teaching, you have forgotten the beginning and when you reach the end of the teaching, you have forgotten the middle part and by the time the teaching is over, you cannot remember anything. So this is called the second fault of the container.

Now we come to the third fault of the container: even if the container is in an upright position and there are no holes underneath, but there is dirt inside, then whatever good things you pour in it, they get spoiled by the dirt and you cannot use them. Similarly if one has faults then it is not good. Therefore not only should the container have the correct upright position with no holes, but it is also important that the container should be clean.

Which are the dirty things? There are six faults: the first one is pride about one's race, pride about one's knowledge, etc. No qualities can remain because of the fault of pride, that is why fault number one is pride.